Self-Bullying: What to Do When the Bully is YOU!

Sherri Strohecker Leopold

Copyright 2019 by Sherri Leopold

Bio Photo by Ed Clark Photography

Cover photos by Victoria Williams and Cheyenne Ellsworth.

All rights preserved. No part of this publication may be reproduced, distributed, or transmitted in any form or by any means, without prior written permission.

Publisher's Note: This is a work of fiction. Names, characters, places, and incidents are a product of the authors experience and/or imagination. Locales and public names are sometimes used for atmospheric purposes. Any resemblance to actual people, living or dead, or businesses, companies, events, institutions, or locales is completely coincidental.

Book Layout and Cover Design by: Eswari Kamireddy

Self-Bullying: What to Do When the Bully is YOU! Sherri Leopold Sherri Leopold

ISBN: 978-1-7331528-0-8 (Paperback)

ISBN: 978-1-7331528-1-5 (eBook)

Dedication

Lovingly Dedicated to:

Paul Charles Strohecker

02/16/31-01/09/18

The greatest gift I have ever received from the Father was my Father. He loved me no matter what and never had an unkind word for anyone even if they deserved one.

This one's for you Dad!

CONTENTS

Foreword	vii
Acknowledgements	ix
About the Author	xii

CHAPTER 1 — 1
What is self-bullying?

CHAPTER 2 — 10
How did we get here and where did the self-bullying start?
Is anyone immune?

CHAPTER 3 — 21
The Prevalence of Self-Bullying and How Easily It Is Accepted By Society

CHAPTER 4 — 30
Put the Bat Down!

CHAPTER 5 — 36
The F.A.R.M Test:
The NEVER fail test to know if you are Self-Bullying

CHAPTER 6 — 42

It is time to SNAP out of it!
Awareness is the Answer

CHAPTER 7 — 51

HELP Me!!
Who are the people closest to you- your inner circle?

CHAPTER 8 — 55

The Power of ME Expressway!

CHAPTER 9 — 66

The Journey to loving who you are
Is this something you can cure?

CHAPTER 10 — 70

YOU ARE A W.O.W. Warrior!

Foreword

I was excited to see Sherri Leopold's book on bullying. "Stop Self-Bullying: What to do when the bully is YOU!" uses today's language of bullying to demonstrate and explain our negative self-talk. In my world, I deal with the subconscious mind and hidden patterns so I can see how wonderfully Sherri connects that with bullying. Not only is this book filled with insights, it also provides the reader with action items to start the process to STOP. This allows the ready to understand that they are not alone, that there is help, and that it is ok to ask for help so that they can begin "The Journey to loving who" they "are." That is crucial and clearly this work is meant for all those who understand the bullying language and are ready to take a step to a better understanding and thereby to a journey to heal and become a "W.O.W. Warrior".

A wonderful work with a "spoonful of sugar" to help us more easily digest the truth about Self Bullying.

Natalie Forest, Ph.D.
Executive Director Women of Global Change

America's Leading Expert in Personal Performance

Thank you for writing such a brilliant book. It's more than a book, it's a life journal!!! It's thought provoking and deep. It really helped me take a good look at myself and how I too sometimes rank myself out by using self-deprecating words in jest. We definitely become the words that we speak if we say them loud enough and long enough.

Thank you for sharing the depth and breadth of how we all tend to use words that we unknowingly become. Thank you for your transparency, love and kindness. Thank you for sharing this with us!

Lisa Ascolese - The Inventress
Speaker, Philanthropist, Inventor, Product Consultant and Agent for Major Television Networks such as QVC, HSN, Evine Live and others.
Founder of AOWIE- Association of Women Inventors and
Entrepreneurs

Acknowledgements

Thank you to my wonderful husband Scott, who has always been my biggest supporter! I should also add editor, shoulder to cry or whine on, handyman, and best all-around guy I know! I will love you until the end of time!

Thank you so much to my 3 children Justin, Josh, and Elizabeth for teaching me so much about being a mom. This movement was born through helping teach you all that you are the boss applesauce on the way to school every day. I am so proud of all of you!

To my best friend Stacey Baxter Bivens- You embody what the word friend means. You are a survivor, a champion, and the best friend a girl could ask for! I love YOU!

To my cherished friend Stacey Frick- I thank you for the nudge to write this book and start this movement. It was in me- you helped bring it out and I am grateful!

Evan Trad- We haven't known each other very long but I would go anywhere with you! Oh the places we'll go… #adventureswithsherriandevan

Dr. Tylisha Johnson- I can't express how grateful I am for your guidance in helping my small idea become an entire movement! Thank you for your Eagle mentorship!

Dr. Cassandra Bradford- I have felt your love and support in this movement from day 1, and I am so thankful for your encouragement.

To the rest of my family- I thank you all for supporting me with all the various projects I have been involved in. I would not be the strong woman I am today without you. If it weren't for my brothers, Steve, Scott, Sheldon, Michael, and my sister Lisa- I wouldn't be the person I am today- so yes it's your fault…lol.

To two of the strongest women I know- My mother Jan and Step-Mother Sondra: while you are very different, I have been blessed with the best mom and best bonus mom a girl could ask for! I love you both with all my heart.

I give all the glory to God for this book. I am thankful for His spirit in me that has poured out onto the page in hopes of creating a better world in which to live. May He see these words as a blessing and in honor of Him!

About the Author

Sherri Strohecker Leopold is a dynamic, multi-gifted, and game-changing powerhouse! She has worked in the Network Marketing/Direct Selling industry for 20 years, gaining experience in speaking, mentoring and team building. Sherri is an Independent Brand Promoter for Le-Vel, a leader in health and wellness industry and currently lives in Springfield IL, USA.

To improve your health and thrive, you may

connect with her at ThrivewithSherri.com

As a thought leader and results-driven veteran in this industry, Sherri remains passionate about encouraging others to live their best life and create financial freedom. She enjoys helping others develop both physical and financial success, and coaches and mentors a large team all over the world.

Sherri is also a gifted writer. She served as contributing editor for the *Healthy Lifestyles* column for *Exposure Magazine* and, as a contributing writer for B.R.A.G. Magazine. Additionally, she co-authored her first book called: *From Grief to Grind* in 2018.

In mid 2018, Sherri also established her own platform called: *Dream BIG with Sherri*, where she shares her gifts with the world through blogging, writing and speaking for organizations and private groups. It doesn't matter how you encounter, and experience Dream BIG with Sherri, you will learn how to love the life you're living, by connecting to and living your BIGGEST dreams!

Outside of business and most importantly, she has been happily married to Scott Leopold for over 31 years. Together, they have three amazing children. She is also a fur mom to five felines and has spent many years helping with feline rescue, through her volunteer services with the Forever Home Feline Ranch. Sherri enjoys writing, reading, painting and drawing in her free time.

God opens doors for those who hold the door open for others! ~Sherri Leopold

You may contact Sherri at:

    DreamBIGwithSherri@gmail.com

or through her website at:

    www.SherriLeopold.com

Speaking engagements may be booked by calling: (636) 692-4415.

CHAPTER 1

What is self-bullying?

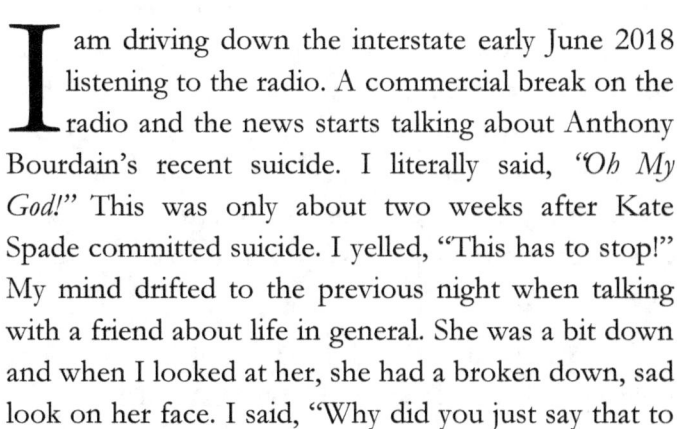

I am driving down the interstate early June 2018 listening to the radio. A commercial break on the radio and the news starts talking about Anthony Bourdain's recent suicide. I literally said, *"Oh My God!"* This was only about two weeks after Kate Spade committed suicide. I yelled, "This has to stop!" My mind drifted to the previous night when talking with a friend about life in general. She was a bit down and when I looked at her, she had a broken down, sad look on her face. I said, "Why did you just say that to yourself?" She looked surprised and said "What?". I said, "Why did you just say I am always broke, nothing good is ever going to happen for me, I am always going to be alone etc.?" She said, "Wow." I asked her if she thought she needed to say those things out loud for someone else to know she was saying them to herself. Hmmm.

Still driving, I repeated out loud, "This has to STOP!"

Remember when I exclaimed: *"Oh My God!"*? God answered my cry with the information contained in this book. This exact moment was where the title of this book was downloaded into my spirit. The title was there before any of the content. It's never changed during the writing process either. My purpose was revealed. He showed me that even someone with the most incredible friends, and family support, the dream job, and all the money you could ever spend in a lifetime, still has the everyday battle with what I call your *IVY* or, your 'inner voice' More on IVY, later....

The next moment I heard clear as day, Self-Bullying: What to do when the Bully is YOU!

I felt an incredible urge so strongly that I had to

DO something! RIGHT NOW!! I needed to act immediately, as if it is a matter of life or death - because for some, it might be.

What happens to all the people who don't have all the needed money, significant others, or great support systems? How can they EVER win at this game of life if the starting point for them is so far behind these people who are taking their life? In that very moment is where the journey to create the movement to stop self-bullying began!

Self-Bullying - What exactly IS self-bullying?

That's an excellent question. It's important we understand what it means first so we understand what we are even talking about. First, let's define the two words separately. It's important to look closely at the meaning of the words:

Self- A person's nature, or character.

Bully- A blustering quarrelsome, overbearing person who habitually badgers and intimidates a smaller or weaker person.

Therefore, one would conclude correctly that self-bullying would be YOU being the overbearing, blustery person who is habitually intimidating and degrading themselves because YOU are the weaker, smaller person.

What? Who does this to themselves?

You. Me. We ALL do it at times to varying degrees. Most people simply aren't aware that this is what they are doing. Maybe because it never had a recognizable name before. We certainly understand what bullying is and how abhorrent and harmful it is to be bullied. I think it's time to shine a light on this issue of self-bullying, and take a look at what we regularly say to ourselves. That "inner voice" that I mentioned earlier, that runs on repeat in our head is what we will be referring to. We will call it *IV* or *Ivy* for easier understanding. We will talk about her a lot. You may have other names for inner voice, but they probably aren't fit for print. IV stands for intravenous. This means literally directly in the vein. Veins run through and sustain every single part of your body. "Inner voice" is wholly responsible for self-bullying. So Ivy fuels your entire being. Whatever is coming in the I.V., affects the entire body and mind. You do control what's coming in the vein. Sometimes it's hard to admit we are guilty of self-bullying because of its self-destructive, demeaning nature. We aren't proud of it; in fact, often we feel completely ashamed.

In this book, we are going to learn how to become an **A.C.E.**:

A. – **Acknowledge** - to acknowledge or accept, take ownership

C. – **Change** - to create something different by choosing different behaviors

E. – **Evolve** - to develop, advance or grow into something new

This acronym represents how you will change this behavior, delivering the strategy to quiet Ivy. This is an ongoing process and journey. You CAN stop this destructive cycle of self-degrading talk. It will take time and patience and grace for you to do it. But it WILL be worth it.

If you are reading this and doubt you self-bully, ask yourself a question. It's a simple yet powerful question. When is the last time you said to yourself:

"Why am I so _____?"

Insert words like, dumb, fat, stupid, skinny, geeky, weird, disorganized, ugly, worthless, etc.

I am sure you're getting the point. It's inevitable; we all do it. Sometimes it is just a flippant comment here or there and sometimes it's burning a hole in your heart. Some people even admire it in others, calling it "self-deprecating humor". Most people can never put a finger on the time they started doing this. I think you will come to understand that it started way earlier than you might think.

Can you list the top 5 things you have said to yourself repeatedly, Ivy's dirty deeds, that weren't positive and affirming?

- First list (1) the negative or offending situation you can recall;
- List (1a) how the actual experiences affected you and how Ivy manifests these in your life today.

1.

_____
_____
_____

1.a

_____
_____
_____

2.

_____
_____
_____

2.a

_____
_____

3.

3.a

4.

4.a

5.

_____
_____
_____

5.a

_____
_____
_____

CHAPTER 2

How did we get here and where did the self-bullying start?
Is anyone immune?

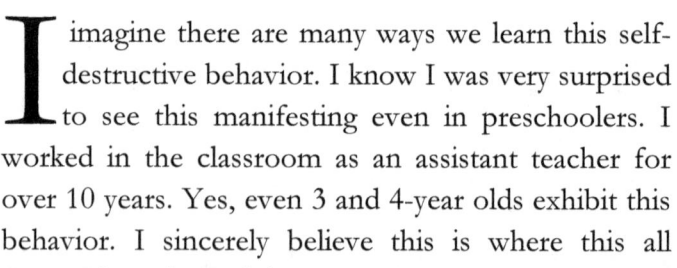

I imagine there are many ways we learn this self-destructive behavior. I know I was very surprised to see this manifesting even in preschoolers. I worked in the classroom as an assistant teacher for over 10 years. Yes, even 3 and 4-year olds exhibit this behavior. I sincerely believe this is where this all starts. I have been doing some digging into this issue.

As I have asked around, I have not been surprised to find it is, in fact, something that starts very young in many cases. We are "gifted" with advice, suggestions, or labels. Call it what you like; the result is the same. I learned this in my own teaching experiences in pre-school.

I assure that neither class, socio-economic status, race, gender, or any other label or characteristic exempts you from this behavior. I want to share a couple examples of two highly successful women, of different races and different backgrounds who had similar self-bullying tendencies. They both overcame it and lead incredibly successful lives. I thank Gloria Macdonald and Dr. Cassandra Bradford for their transparency and courage in sharing so that you, too, may know it can be done!

The first story is from Gloria Macdonald, who is a very successful entrepreneur, leader, and speaker, who has made it her mission to help others succeed in the Network Marketing industry with her mentoring and training materials. Maybe you can relate to her story.

Gloria Macdonald's story:

"My brother, who is two years older than

me, and who I adore, is sitting on the living room floor building an incredible fort with his special stacking blocks.

I am so excited to play with him that I go bounding over, in my clumsy little 3-yr-old body. I trip, fall on his fort and demolished it. My brother starts screaming and me and telling me how stupid I am.

I know it's true because I see it over and over again. He can color in the lines, I can't.

He can make the blocks balance, I can't.

He can read those signs, I can't.

So I make the decision that I AM stupid and not good enough.

And I spend all my energy trying to prove to myself and everyone else that I'm not stupid and that I am good enough.

I become the classic overachiever in everything…

At school, at work, even at play.

Fast forward 50 years and I've been an overachiever my whole life.

I've worked like <u>mad</u> to create a multiple 7 figure business and a life I love, and prove to myself and everyone else that I'm <u>not</u> stupid. I <u>am</u> smart and capable.

I come home from a two-week vacation in Italy with my husband to find out, through a series of circumstances…

Everything I've worked my whole life to create, is literally gone overnight. The business is gone.

I have hundreds of thousands of dollars of expenses and salaries to pay and absolutely no income.

We ended up having to cash in every dime of retirement savings we had, I racked up tens of thousands of dollars of credit card debt, we were forced to sell our home, and we came razor close to having to declare bankruptcy…

This all really happened.

At first it was very difficult to talk about.

Let's be honest…

I wouldn't admit this to anyone.

Now though, I can talk about this without the pain associated with these events.

I can do it because things have changed.

And no matter where you are on your journey...

They can change for you too.

But you have to start with taking the first step.

After MONTHS of struggle...

And scraping together every last penny of credit I could, to invest tens of thousands of dollars in training to learn how to grow a network marketing business online...

With little success, and mostly more failure...

I just couldn't go on losing $2 - $3,000/mo on Facebook ads.

FINALLY, There Was A HUGE Turning Point.

I created one highly successful business. I wasn't stupid. I never was. I was just two years younger than my brother. My parents loved me. They always did. And I was always enough.

If I'd done it once, I could do it again. I knew I would be able to reinvent myself...

And I decided I wanted to dedicate myself to helping other people create change and breakthroughs in their lives."

Gloria Macdonald has helped thousands of people create the business they want through her strategies and marketing techniques, especially through Linkedin. She chose to stand in and embrace her power and control her words. She IS a warrior, that warrior you will learn about shortly.

The next story is from Dr. Cassandra Bradford, the CEO and Founder of Genesis Preferred and the Founder of the Run Women's Conference. She is a business coach, a strategist, leader, writer, and speaker. She has been a true inspiration to me in my life and business since the day I met her in early 2018. Imagine my surprise when this topic resonated with her. I asked her to share her story, a story of growth.

Dr. Cassandra Bradfords Story:

> "Growing up in a home with mostly brothers can be difficult. It seems almost normal or acceptable for your big brother to "pick" on you, break your baby dolls, or even prevent you from having a boyfriend. In my home, the issue wasn't that I was the youngest, or the smartest, or the cutest—my issues

were that I was the darkest and fattest.

My history was that I was raised by bi-racial parents who had me late in life. They discovered entrepreneurship late in life as well. By the time I was born, my parents were in their mid-40's and discovered the demands a small business adds to a stressful family, let alone the time to deal with the cries from their youngest child.

Most of my childhood, I was overweight and the darkest one in my family. I was constantly reminded that I didn't fit or that I didn't look like everyone else in the family. Being called "chubby" or "tar-baby" were hurtful and harmful. I questioned my birth constantly with my parents who shrugged my concerns as "big brothers-little sister" syndrome. For me, it created deep rooted scars that haunted me most of my childhood and early teen years. I wasn't accepted by my aunts, uncles, or cousins because of the color of my skin. The constant reminder caused me to either want to starve myself or over-eat. Even when others would ask me about my family, I would make up stories that I was from two Black parents who loved to cook (though they did own a restaurant) so that it would not raise suspicion. I would grieve deeply that I wasn't accepted by family, or even my community.

It wasn't until I moved to California to go to college, where everyone was beautifully tanned and physically fit, that I melted into my new acceptance of myself. I began to work out (so I could fit in) and lay out under the warm sun rays with my new-found friends where I turned a beautiful caramel brown color and became toned enough to compete in fitness competitions.

I understand self-bullying in the deepest sense. I was ostracized by those who loved me and from the world who didn't because of the color of my skin and the size of my body. I even withdrew from my family and friends who knew my family personally, because I didn't want to be asked questions as to why I looked differently from them. I helped them along this journey by allowing the ridicule to continue. Now, I enjoy the color of my skin and the dark hue I receive when kissed by the sun. I also enjoy every inch of my curves as they represent who I am.

I am ME...Dr. Cass."

Self-bullying weighs thousands of pounds in our minds. We can't escape it. Those words are a crushing weight to a tiny 3 or 4 year old's mind. It creates wounds that run deep and leave lasting scars. If you know anything about scar tissue, it's not very flexible. In fact it is kind of stuck right where it is. This is what happens when we are "self-bullying" in love, hate or any other emotion. We are wounded, cut deep. We are sometimes too young to remember the actual words, but the words do leave lasting marks and scars. Most people shy away from pain at any cost. We will avoid situations where the wound is reopened or disturbed. Sometimes that means avoiding people or places, jobs, or promotions, just like Dr. Cassandra did. Seriously, who really wants to rip a scab off or tear into a scar, even if it is uncomfortable the way it is? The only way to remove scar tissue it to cut it out! If we don't, the result is less than stellar. We don't want to move, because it hurts, or is uncomfortable. We become hemmed in and stuck by the scar tissue. Many times it's years and years of wounds piling on top of one another. It isn't just the inflexibility of scar tissue, it's the emotional weight of it also.

If I am 3 years old, sitting in the sandbox and another 3-year-old comes up to me and says "get out of the sandbox you can't play here!" or "I don't like your red hair and those weird spots on your face." (insert your personal defining characteristic; ugly, black, fat, asian, tall, skinny, short, little - you get it!) Will I then spend the rest of my life dying my hair and bleaching my skin, or using full coverage makeup to avoid letting the spots or freckles show? Will I be trying to mentally separate myself from that painful event where I felt "less than"? Because, in reality, I was beautifully and wonderfully made by God, right? Hence the conflicted feelings.

As an adult, I may not even remember the exact incident. However, I may feel very strongly about not wanting to have red hair and freckles. I.V. continues to disturb the wounds and bump the healing scabs. Scars tend to last forever, unless we remove them. Surgery does seem drastic though, huh?

Can you recall the earliest memory you have of feeling "less than"?

_____
_____
_____
_____
_____
_____
_____
_____
_____
_____

How does this feel today when thinking about it? Do you have scars?

_____
_____
_____
_____
_____
_____
_____
_____
_____

CHAPTER 3

The Prevalence of Self-Bullying and How Easily It Is Accepted By Society

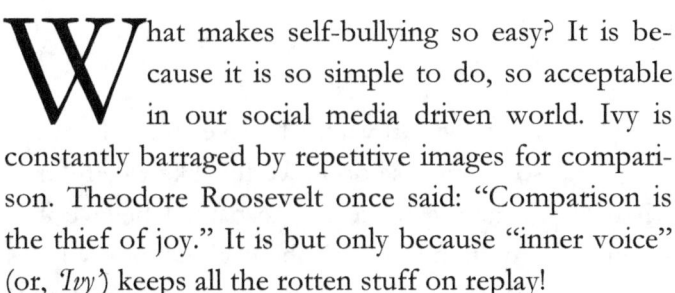

What makes self-bullying so easy? It is because it is so simple to do, so acceptable in our social media driven world. Ivy is constantly barraged by repetitive images for comparison. Theodore Roosevelt once said: "Comparison is the thief of joy." It is but only because "inner voice" (or, *Ivy*) keeps all the rotten stuff on replay!

You all have people you know who constantly post things on social media about how they aren't worth anything, life sucks, and every other negative way of describing their existence. We run to their defense immediately. A quick pick-me-up, cheer-up or, *you are awesome* message, is usually what follows. But have you ever challenged that person to quit self-bullying? I have! I encourage you to do the same, privately, of course. We aren't aiming to wound them again or rip a scab off. Simply encourage them to challenge their "inner voice"!

We have to come to a place of awareness and acknowledgement if we ever hope to overcome self-bullying. Society as a whole actually loves self-bullying as a concept. It is in every single movie, book, play, television show, etc. We are always excited when someone overcomes a challenge or a down moment, but that doesn't change the fact we like to see it. Sounds weird, right?

In some very odd way, I believe this is because, if we hear someone else do it, we feel like we are okay when we do it. We relate to the pain. I believe it is summed up quite nicely with the cliché' "misery loves company". Remember that *like* does attract *like*. If you are miserable and hating on yourself, look around you and see who your circle of influence is. When you look at them do you see the best part of yourself or do you see a negative version of yourself? We will talk about this more in chapter 8 when we will discuss your personal tribe or friend circle. The most watched videos on all social media and YouTube will be those who have shown someone who was in a tough spot and rose up and conquered. Have you ever looked at a video and read the hateful comments people make? A "famous person" had it handed to them, or of course they look like that because they are rich, or have a trainer, or a chef, or whatever. Even more fascinating, is that people will argue and insult one another with in the comments! This has become socially acceptable. Throwing hate onto people you have never met, or do not know, or even understand their circumstances has become commonplace. My friend and author SharRon Jamison's comment comes to mind. She says: "*The higher the level, the higher the devil!*" She was speaking on what happens when you work to improve yourself, elevate your circumstances, improve your looks, get a higher level job, whatever the case may be, and the people who initially cheered you on are now criticizing you, and your efforts. Essentially a good vs. evil battle. When you become famous, or are thrown into the spotlight for some reason, people take it upon themselves to try to "bring you down a notch." This is a very challenging concept that is hard to fully understand, let alone accept. It's ironic, honestly. One must simply acknowledge and know that people will respond to you from exactly where they stand in their own life. Misery loves company, and your success won't always cheered on the same way, but it should be. Truly successful people ALWAYS cheer other peoples' successes. Miserable people rarely honestly cheer successful people, as it exposes their own perceived weaknesses and enhances their self-bullying tendencies. This is something you will need to understand along your journey. Accepting this can be a lonely part of your growth process.

People, especially family and friends, expect you to behave and act in a certain manner. When you STOP self-bullying, and no longer allow yourself to be bullied by others (setting clear boundaries and expectations), they will not always respond well. It is literally about keeping the status quo, even when it doesn't serve you. You need to understand that if you change your own behavior and act differently, people around you are forced to respond to you in a different way. This forced response is not of their doing.

The Prevalence of Self-Bullying and How Easily It Is Accepted By Society

Consider this scenario. You go to a party, where you would normally slink in with your partner/best friend, do very little mingling, and look down most of the time. Perhaps your companion is very talkative and more outgoing. What if, instead, YOU choose the opportunity to reinvent yourself and become the person who wants to meet everyone in the room? You boldly introduce yourself to people and carry on conversations to the very end. Upon leaving, your friend/partner says to you in the car. "Wow, you sure were talkative tonight!" Immediately, your whole being starts to shut down and you start thinking, "Did people think I talked too much, did I seem silly? I should have stayed home or not said anything." However; the real question is "what did the question even mean"? Were they actually thrilled that you were so outgoing? Did they feel upstaged, or not as valued? Did they not know how to relate to you when you acted differently than expected? It could be any one of those. It is very important how you respond, because here is where you can change the pattern. If your response is, "Yes, I decided to show up with my true inside showing, and it was so fun and I loved it!" then you have affirmed that this is how you wanted to act, and that you were very happy with the result. You have your foot firmly planted on the baseball bat. (We will discuss this bat in the next chapter at length.)

I do feel that it's very important to disclose to your inner circle when you embark on this empowerment journey. They should expect changes, and not be surprised when you put your "brave" on and rediscover and reinvent yourself. It gives you the power to remind them, this is WHO you are, and you are growing and changing in many positive ways. Ways that are positive to YOU! They can deal with it or not. This journey is between you and your Higher Power. Anyone else's opinion is highly overrated, AND none of your business.

We have to learn to set boundaries for our friends, family, and even spouses and parents, as well as for all of society. Step into your personal power knowing full well it may not be received perfectly by others who are important to you. However, at the end of the day, you are MOST important to you! Whether self-bullying is socially accepted or not doesn't matter. It doesn't matter if everyone does it, or that you feel justified in doing it because of your circumstances. It will NEVER be the correct thing to invest your time and energy in- EVER! There will never be a good return on investment when you spend your time and energy doing it. At the end of the day, you need to have a full bank account of positive and supportive people, energy, and influences, no matter what the cost. You are simply worth any amount of confusion, distress or challenge.

Becky from *yourmodernfamily.com* states in an article referring to raising her children:

"I understand that our words become their inner voices and I try to work hard to say things

that I want them to really know." That's so powerful!

As you may also remember from *The Help*, Abilene says, "You is kind. You is smart. You is important!" This is fact, people. Own it! Our words have massive power!

It's time to harness your POWER!

Let us identify some areas of our life that we allow others people's perceptions, words, judgements, or opinions impact how we view ourselves.

Social Circle:

_____
_____
_____
_____
_____
_____
_____
_____
_____

Personal Relationships:

_____
_____
_____
_____
_____
_____
_____
_____

Workplace or career:

_____
_____
_____
_____
_____
_____
_____
_____
_____

CHAPTER 4

Put the Bat Down!

Remember the bat I referred to? Yes, it's there. There is a figurative baseball bat that lays at each person's feet no matter who you are. You are oblivious to it being there. As in the previous example about red hair and freckles, that was where you became aware of it. I refer to that as being hit with the baseball bat for the first time. OUCH!

At the end of the last chapter, I asked you to identify some areas of your life, where you allowed judgements or opinions to impact how you view yourself. It is YOUR first realization that the bat exists. The hits hurt, leave a mark and are generally unpleasant. I am certain we are all born with this bat simply on the ground at our feet. We are completely unaware it's even there until someone picks it up and uses it on us. We can't see other peoples' bat or our own, until we are made aware of it. Often, our bat is shown to us by people who love us. Our parents, siblings, close friends or grandparents are the first to pick it up and make a mark. It doesn't mean they don't love us, sometimes they think it's just "teaching us" something. "It will make you tough, or strong!"

The problem is that this bat is picked up by others, used and dropped at our feet when they turn and walk away. The first bully you encounter makes you aware it's there. Until that moment, we were unfamiliar with the bat. However; now we know it there. Now, we happily pick it up and continue beating the different words that have been placed on it by others, into our being. We take it all in. Even though only we can see them, they gain power in repeating them. Each time we retell the offending event to someone, that's another self-hit, and we repeat the self-bullying words to ourselves by re-telling others. Ivy is having a fine time! Every time we replay it in our mind, we hit ourselves again and repeat the words. Each time we try to reason through it, we hit ourselves again. We repeat the words, which by repeating, we accept ownership of it.

For example; "He isn't interested in me, he probably hates my ugly freckles too."

BAM! This is why self-bullies are so battered, bruised and scarred. We willingly pick up the discarded bat they left behind with offending words and continue to abuse ourselves by replaying offending events to all who will listen. Sometimes we think of it as venting, and sometimes it's just needing someone to tell us we are okay. The original bully might be a parent, grandparent, spouse or friend.

Know the first offender can easily be someone who loves us too. Once you are aware of its existence at your feet, anyone can pick it up and beat you with it, AND you can beat yourself with it over and over too. You begin to appear to others with what seems like a blinking sign over your head that says:

"go ahead, pick the bat up, write some words, take a swing, I deserve it".

Not everyone will pick it up, though. Those people who do feel less than (also self-bullies), will see it as an opportunity to relate to you from where they are. They will draw you right into their pain spiral and give you a good whack with own your bat.

Remember, they have their own bat at their feet as well and it has hurtful words on it too. It's just that it helps them feel MORE powerful to hit you with your bat!

Their bat seems much smaller, insignificant and less painful as they hit you with yours. It is truly how bullies are built. It is a perpetual cycle that turns itself inward. It just doesn't hurt as much if you can keep doing it to someone else. You don't have to think about your own pain when you inflict some on others.

The great news is you CAN put the bat down at any time! Once you understand and acknowledge that you do self-bully, you are on your way to becoming an A.C.E.(mentioned in chapter 1), because you now will be aware enough to change it.

First step will be to stand up, step forward and put your foot on the bat with all your weight and declare "NO MORE!" I like to say, "No thank you, I don't receive that!" Draw a line in the sand, create a boundary, think of yourself in a bubble. Whatever thought process you need to use to think of yourself wrapped in an insulator and a protective barrier - do it. Your protective space around you is in your control. When we control this space and control the people, we let in around us, we will move forward unharmed. The places we frequent, both in mind and body, and how we outwardly present ourselves to others will improve our lives even more.

Most times self-bullying people feel a total lack of control over everything in their lives. All people go through difficult times, these times will present as your stressors or triggers for a self-assault.

What are some areas in your life that you feel a lack of control?

_____
_____
_____
_____
_____
_____
_____
_____

What are your stressors or triggers?

_____
_____
_____
_____
_____
_____
_____
_____

CHAPTER 5

The F.A.R.M Test:
The NEVER fail test to know if you are Self-Bullying

Up to this point, you have probably said oh maybe I do that sometimes. Perhaps you thought "Wow I do that ALL the time every day!"

There is a very simple test to know for sure; I call it the F.A.R.M. test:

THE F.A.R.M TEST: *THE NEVER FAIL TEST TO KNOW IF YOU ARE SELF-BULLYING*

F - Friends
A - And
R - Relatives (natural, step, fosters, adopted, all of them)
M – Matter

It means that Friends *and* Relatives Matter. They DO!

Imagine sitting directly across from your best friend, mom, daughter, father, grandmother or child. You look them directly in the eye and repeat what just went through your own head or what came out of your mouth, but in the form of *you*, instead of *I*. For example, "You are so fat. You are *so* stupid. Why do you attract terrible people?" Can you even imagine saying that out loud to someone you love?!

You are probably appalled at the thought of even saying this to your mom or your 13 or 15-year-old daughter or granddaughter. Yet it is quite easy to hit yourself with that bat. But it makes you cringe to think of taking that bat and hitting someone you love with it.

Do you love yourself? If so, why can you so easily hurt yourself, yet feel terrible about the thought of doing it to someone else? It boils down to worthiness and value.

Do you value yourself BELOW all others you care about? Isn't that like handing the bat to anyone who wants to take a swing?

The F.A.R.M test is fairly simple and easy to understand. The bottom line is this; if you won't say it out loud to someone else's face, or someone on the F.A.R.M., don't say it to yourself!

Your outcome will change dramatically, depending on who your allies are. The duration of time it takes you to accomplish your mission of standing in the POWER OF ME, will be directly affected by who you partner with along the way. Many people speak of these people as your tribe, your vibe, friends, posse, or even ride or die. It is not important what you call them, but WHO they are!

These must be people who are willing to SNAP(more in chapter 6) you, accept a SNAP from you, support you, encourage you, and cheer you on at all times! They will accept your chosen destination, support your plan, and provide necessary things along the way. It might be a hug, a card of encouragement, a well-placed SNAP, a social media share of your accomplishments, or even a conversation to expand your horizon.

Identify The most important people on your F.A.R.M. and the impact they have made in your life. Identify them with the related experience and how they affect you.

Negative FARM Members:

_____
_____
_____
_____
_____
_____
_____
_____
_____

Positive and Affirming FARM Members:

_____
_____
_____
_____
_____
_____
_____
_____

How are you showing up on other people's FARM?

_____
_____
_____
_____
_____
_____
_____

This is where I am known to say repeatedly: Make good choices friends! How you show up on someone else's FARM is very important. The cliché your vibe will attract your tribe is the real deal!

CHAPTER 6

It is time to SNAP out of it!
Awareness is the Answer

Guess what? It's time to POWER UP and SNAP out of it! YES! You CAN! There is hope in overcoming this. As I did in Chapter 1, I will be showing you how to become an A.C.E. in this chapter as well.

Remember: A.C.E. stands for Acknowledge, Change, and Evolve.

We need to **Acknowledge** that we bully ourselves. **Change** the behavior and **Evolve** into a better version of ourselves. No one is immune. We all do it at one time or another and many of us do it every day, all day long.

I have three older brothers that were often quick to tease when I was young. This caused me to use self-deprecating humor a lot. It is a defense mechanism to poke fun at yourself first before anyone else can... also known as self-bullying. There is generally a thread of truth running through that kind of humor, based on how you really feel. I will share a personal story with you.

It's a silly story from when I was working in the pre-school. One of the little girls came up to the lead teacher and I, and said proudly "I am going to have a princess birthday party at the swimming pool, and you are both invited!" I said "awesome! I will come as the Princess of Wales/Whales". The other teacher burst out laughing, and the child said, "Silly Sherri".

You see, I DID think it was really funny, but the truth was, the other teacher was very slender, an avid runner, and often ate twice what I did (especially sweets). Given that I was around this lead teacher 5 days/week, she was who I compared my body to each day. She also was and is one of the most stylish women I know. She is also very kind and loving. I never received any body shaming messages from her- it was me.

So the thread of truth running through that scenario is that I was judging my body harshly. Perhaps my saving grace was that I didn't feel "less than" simply because there is more of me for people to see. Not everyone can say that. Most people are saying hateful things to themselves daily. Yes, I did say daily. Body shaming is just one common way to perpetuate self-bullying.

In my conversations for this book, I have discovered that it is true that many of these patterns develop early on, or as a response to an earlier experience. If you are a parent, you begin to realize that those experiences then bleed right on to our children as well, and then they form the same opinions of themselves. I will be creating some parenting tools in the future to prevent this.

My own extended family has a little girl in it who is already making statements like, "I don't ever want to be fat". When asked: "Why do you say that, honey, you are just fine the way you are", she replies: "I can't get fat; it's not good". Already, at six years old, she has specific ideas about body image. These are not ideas that come naturally to a six-year-old.

Many questions came to mind after hearing that. How will this manifest itself when she deals with the body changes that come with puberty? If she decides to have a child many years from now, how will she feel about her body? If you have given birth, is everything in the same place? Likely not.

Do you see how this self-bullying is carried into our adulthood, and into our mental thought patterns? How our words bleed all over and contaminate people around us? I am not EVEN talking YET about what we attract when we talk to ourselves BADLY! What sort of people do you think you will attract if you are constantly saying "oh, I am so stupid, broke, or even broken? I am nothing...." You will attract exactly what you act like.

You will NATURALLY attract those who confirm for you that you are nothing. It should be apparent that while we DO bully ourselves, it is NOT producing an awesome outcome.

I am going to provide you with an incredible tool you can implement to stop self-bullying, create a pact with your tribe to stop, and help create a movement that promotes loving ourselves more. It's called S.N.A.P. This is an acronym with a double meaning; meaning it has 2 sets of words. I am going to teach it to you. YOU will be able to teach it to others. You WILL be able to ask people to help you catch yourself if you are self-bullying!

This is a way for you to have a cue to help you **Change** the behavior after you have **Acknowledge (d)** it so you can **Evolve**!

The Acronym: SNAP

S- Speaking: words and I.V.

S- Start: do it immediately

N- Negatively: anything that creates a yucky feeling

N- NOW: at this moment in time

A- Attracts: anything that draws something to you

A- Activating: to make something active or operate

P- Pain/Poop: anything that hurts or stinks

P- Power: the capacity to direct or influence the behavior of others or the course of events

Now that you have the words we will learn how it works. Start with your NON dominant hand. NON dominant means it should NOT be in charge! Snap with me with your non dominant hand saying each word with a single snap of the hand each one for a total of four snaps.

S. Speaking
N. Negatively
A. Attracts
P. Poop/Pain

What do we know about poop or pain? No one likes it, no one wants it, and no one wants to be around it because it STINKS or HURTS!

So let's put our dominant hand up snap with me the same way, saying:

S. Start
N. Now
A. Activating
P. Power

THIS is what we want! Here's how you use this: If you are the person who will use this frequently (I hope you are!), you enlist the people close to you, the tribe we will talk about, to help catch you. Teach them to just snap until you stop talking negatively and rephrase what you are saying in a positive loving way. You can do it when you are by yourself, too. After having heard this, you will be more aware, and just like when you or your spouse is pregnant, you see all the pregnant ladies everywhere… you will hear the self-bullying now that you are aware of it. You will also catch yourself doing it. Simply thinking about snapping and thinking about the two sets of four words will redirect your train of thought. It will work every single time.

I imagine all the people who can be saved from themselves by creating and nurturing the movement of simply speaking nicer to ourselves. If we teach our preschoolers to speak kindly to themselves, imagine how different they will be as adults. I ask YOU to read this today; how different would YOU be if you had learned how to redirect those speaking patterns years ago?

PLEASE practice. Memorize the acronyms. They are incredibly powerful! Teach them to anyone who will listen! We can change the world one SNAP at a time! This is what we want more of! It can be heard around my house with my husband and me. Just last week we both "said" SNAP to each other; didn't even have to SNAP. That's when you know you have gotten REALLY good at it. Start NOW Activating power! And I did!

Who will these people be? Are they FARM members? Can you commit to sharing the SNAP as the gift it is? When you hear someone self-bullying- will you-impart this wisdom to them? It will help create the movement to a nicer, kinder, happier world!

What 2 people come to mind who you can teach the SNAP to who will not only benefit from it but who will partner with you to keep you both in check?

1._____

2._____

When you are working on creating the BEST version of yourself, consider the SNAP like making a spark that will start a fire! This SNAP ignites the POWER OF ME! Your abilities and possibilities will be limitless. With your foot firmly planted on the bat, and your SNAP firmly in place, it's time to create the beautiful life you deserve with ALL the right people!

CHAPTER 7

HELP Me!!
Who are the people closest to you-your inner circle?

We have touched on this briefly but I believe it should be discussed more fully. We rarely achieve anything solely by ourselves. You will never become an ACE and eventually a WOW Warrior if you don't stop and take an assessment of who is in your personal space regularly. Who are the people in your inner circle? These people affect your life greatly. Your inner circle's voices often become **YOUR** inner voice. Make good choices.

Since we have designated where we are going, how we will get there and the landmarks that will tell us our path is correct, it important to discuss who will be surrounding us in our journey. These people will reveal themselves to you because they will ALWAYS be the ones who challenge you to be more, do more, create more, and love yourself exactly as you are, just like they do. They do not give you material to write on your bat for future hits. If they do so inadvertently, they will ALWAYS apologize, own it, and make the attempt to erase what they wrote.

This select group of cherished individuals may be one or two or 15. There isn't a correct number of these people, but rather a correct number of attributes they possess that will serve you on your journey. It is also very important that you have clearly defined attributes needed for the people imperative to your journey. These attributes may be things like: honesty, directness, kindness, an attitude of gratitude, trustworthiness, loyalty, or whatever speaks to your heart and mind.

Knowing which characteristics are most important will help you more easily identify who is allowed into your inner circle. Can you list your top 10 most important characteristics a member of your tribe will possess?

_____
_____
_____
_____
_____
_____
_____
_____
_____
_____
_____
_____
_____
_____
_____
_____
_____
_____
_____
_____

Who are the people in your tribe, friendship circle, or whatever you refer to it as that support you 100% at all times and in all ways?

_____
_____
_____
_____
_____

Create your list now that you have listed what characteristics identify them. If the list seems tiny or no one fits the bill, think about expanding your circle of acquaintances.

_____
_____
_____
_____
_____
_____
_____
_____

But wait! Now that we know who we can count on, where are we going? And how do we get there? The Power of ME Expressway!

CHAPTER 8

The Power of ME Expressway!

Success land - Oh the Places We Can go!

Today we are going to talk about taking a trip and staying in your lane. A trip to Success land via the Power of Me Expressway.

I want to share with you some insights into how to make that journey on the road to success. I am using Success land as a place that exists in which you no longer self-bully and love yourself in the extreme. It is NOT a fantasy land. It is a place perhaps you just haven't been before. I will parallel this to taking an actual trip. The journey/road to standing inside your personal power. The Power of ME. Embracing who you truly are requires planning and consistent action.

When you decide to take a trip, you first have to decide where you are going. In other words, you must set a goal or destination and formulate a plan: with the plan being, to loving ourselves just as we are today and embracing our personal strengths. Now, this might be different for each person. It might be accepting what we look like, or loving ourselves at the weight we are, curves and all. It could also mean to excel at our current job, even though it may not be our ideal.

We ARE the vehicle. Check if there is anyone in your vehicle with you!

If someone is in your vehicle, do an inspection on THEM! Are they equipped to be on this journey with you? Will they support you, give direction if the road gets bumpy, help you read the signs, remind you to fill your tank, and to stay in your lane? If they can't handle the duties of that, you will have to leave them behind on this journey. Simply wish them well and tell them you can send them a map at a later time if they want to follow you! DO NOT BACK UP OR OUT

FOR ANYONE! No back-seat drivers allowed, but you will need help along the way which will speak more about shortly.

On your journey, there will be plenty of times you will need to refuel your vehicle, eat, or do maintenance, and you'll encounter some detours or even construction zones (otherwise known as distractions). It doesn't change the fact that we know where we want to go.

When we know where we want to end up, we lay out a plan to get there. Do you want to be a nurse, a doctor, a speaker, or a mom? Love yourself, because all of these things require a proper plan of execution. It is our map, so to speak. It is our goal. We are going to start our trip by having our car (that would be us, because we are the vehicle driving the adventure) in working order, full of fuel (i.e., excitement, motivation, knowledge, employment, etc.) before we take off. Now it would be perfect if we just arrive there without incident. As a general rule though, the trip takes a bit more effort than that, and sometimes things occur that can get us lost or off track.

I want to share with you some of the most common distractions, and some ways to avoid them on your journey to Success land. By the way, the capital of this fine land is No-self-bullying. Consider these helpful tips as you construct your map: whether your trip is to Doctor state, stay-at-home mom state, pay-off-your debt state, or wherever it is you want to go. The first thing to remember when you begin your journey on the road to your success is ALWAYS stay in YOUR lane. You ARE the vehicle and YOU DO control the vehicle. You are driving your life and you determine where it goes. However; there is a reason there are lines on the road for you to stay between. You know, the white and yellow ones that are painted there as guidelines. You already know that double yellow lines are a warning. You can't see fully, so make good choices.

Sometimes there are people in lanes next to you. One of the most difficult challenges in your life will be when someone in your network, friend circle or family "appears" to be passing you or going faster than you. It may appear like they are reaching a successful place faster than you. Their achievements may even appear "better" than yours. But if you focus on them in the other lane, you will start drifting that way. Before you know it, you will be in the ditch, or in the wrong lane with traffic headed towards you, wondering how you got there. The self-bullying talk flows freely in these areas. Even worse yet, you could accidentally rear end or side swipe them with your attitude, and knock them off course too! Yikes! We drive towards whatever we focus on…so remember to stay the course and follow your own map. Focus on your goals (STAY in YOUR lane), not on other "people" or vehicles, or their goals. Theirs may be different than yours.

It is also important to point out that sometimes people will side swipe us and push us towards the ditch for our own good, because they "love" us. They want to save us from ourselves, and to have us follow their plan or their map instead of ours. Surely, they know what's best for you. They might be a good friend, spouse or even a significant other or loved one. In home-based businesses or network marketing, it might sound like this: "no one makes money at that; I heard it's a pyramid scheme; a scam; they make you buy lots of stuff; the economy sucks; you probably shouldn't do this; no one is buying extra stuff these days…" and on and on…

Through it all, you must STAY in your lane and follow YOUR plan. Let them know you appreciate their opinion VERY much, but, if they cannot be positive and supportive of YOUR plan, mutually agree to not talk about it at all. If that is not possible, you may have to put them outside your immediate circle of people to spend time with for a short time. You have to eliminate this negative energy, as it is much like a construction zone filled with cones and shifting lanes. You will be slowed down and perhaps forced off an exit ramp when it wasn't where you wanted to go in the first place.

If your destination is still Success land, you have to keep going. The POWER OF ME awaits your arrival! Say you're on a trip to Florida, and you hit a detour, or a construction zone. Do you decide to go to Texas instead? NO! You continue to follow your map. Stay in your lane, follow YOUR plan. If you do hit a detour, go around it. Adjust and keep going, it doesn't change the destination. No matter how many times you have to adjust, stay the course! Put it in 4 wheel drive if you need to get through the rough spots, but keep your eye on the goal: your destination. Find a way to stay on track, stay in your lane, follow your map, and you'll keep moving forward.

Another caution is to check that your vehicle is

in good working order. If the brakes are not working, your wheels are out of alignment, or your tires are low on pressure, your vehicle can behave unexpectedly, putting you and your journey at risk. Maybe you'll swerve, going off the road, or into oncoming traffic, as you travel down the road to Success land. Things that can affect the operation of your vehicle and eventually cause you to crash show up as backbiting, jealousy, broken friendships, people who are not reliable, lying, spouses cheating, and any number of other awful things. All of these are fuel for self-bullying, not fuel for your vehicle to reach Success land. If you aren't prepared for it, you can be stopped cold. Every single person following you- will rear end you and be stopped as well. It is a chain reaction you can't afford as a leader, parent, or as a friend. It WILL happen if you do not stay focused and stay in your lane! You <u>will</u> pre-plan and think this through if you truly want to get to your destination: Success land. Your journey destination doesn't change with obstacles, detours or potholes; stay in your lane, stay the course, and follow your map. Feel free to revisit your goal of where you want to go occasionally to make sure it is a good one, but don't change it based on detours or obstacles. You are the driver, remember?

By the way, use your rearview mirror sparingly. Looking into it too often or too long is simply living in the past. It is hard to drive forward if you are always looking behind you.

The rearview mirror is an evaluation tool for safety, <u>NOT</u> a navigation tool for blazing a trail forward!

Read that sentence again.

We aren't going backwards. Check in with yourself from time to time, to see if you are looking into the past too often or too long. You will find yourself repeating all the wrong words. Who cares if last month, or the last three months, were not great personally or professionally. If you continue to focus on it, and you can bet there will only be <u>more</u> of the same.

The other AWESOME thing about this journey is that along the way, you will have plenty of landmarks and signs to help guide you in the right direction. These signs will be such things as feeling happier, developing better relationships, attracting the right people both personally and professionally, and so on. You will see bigger numbers on your paycheck, better friends, and a higher level of personal satisfaction, indicating that your map is, in fact, a good one. You may see promotions or raises, more invitations to social events, or people in general commenting on how amazing you look. Or even are!

As you continue driving toward Success land, you will experience bumps in the road, detours, some roadkill (relationships that needed to go to the wayside), and even some people speeding by you doing 90 instead of 70. But none of those things will matter at all to you, if you follow your own journey/map to Success land. Your journey will be powered by your own personal map filled with positive self-talk, love, grace, and determination.

As you journey to Success land, let's discover some of our challenges:

What have you been looking at too long in your rear-view mirror that is holding you back from fully stepping on the gas?

_____
_____
_____
_____
_____
_____
_____
_____

_____

Identify what some of your detours and potholes have been or are along the way.

_____
_____
_____
_____
_____
_____
_____
_____

How can you use this information you identified to clear the way to navigate and blaze a trail towards your destination?

_____
_____
_____
_____
_____
_____
_____
_____
_____

Determine your destination, lay out your plan to get there, declare your personal map, stay in your lane, stay the course and I will see each of you in Success land via the Power of Me Expressway!!

CHAPTER 9

The Journey to loving who you are
Is this something you can cure?

The journey to ending self-bullying can seem long and arduous. No one is immune and it cannot be fully cured. However; it can be controlled! Loving yourself is a precursor to every good thing that can possibly happen in your life! Conversely, if you do not love yourself, or accept yourself as God made you, you will never be completely available or compatible for someone else. This is true for friendships, family and significant other relationships! If I walk up to you bleeding and broken, and wrap my arms around you, you are now going to be covered in something less than desirable. If we stay together long enough and you are empathic enough, you will be broken and bleeding too. Misery loves company, remember?

There are several steps to loving yourself. The first step is to add non-toxic, loving, and encouraging people to your circle. If you feel those characteristics you wrote down in the exercise in chapter 8 don't describe you now, yet do describe what you want to be, choose those people anyway.

Elevate your friends, and you will elevate yourself! Dream of a life where each person who comes into your personal space is filled with positive energy and is living life in a grateful way. Plan to walk into other people's space exactly the same way. God made you exactly who you are, exactly the way you are. There is absolutely no one else like you. You are a snowflake! Literally no two alike. Embrace your individuality, the way you look and how you feel. It's uniquely you. You will NEVER be perfect, but you will always be PERFECTLY YOU!

The second step is to create the life you love living. When you wake up you can affirm out loud, "I

LOVE MY LIFE and I LOVE ME!" We hear so much about positive affirmations being the current "in" thing, or even a passing fad. But here's the reality; positive affirmations work because you are saying "I receive this".

This is also why self-bullying must be stopped. When you say something to yourself, you are affirming your ownership of it. This is why it's a life-long journey. Some days will days will be a breeze; like you are on top of the world. Others, well, not so much. We aren't cured of self-bullying ever. We can, however, minimize the number of occurrences with patience and practice.

You will find that when you **Acknowledge** you are doing it, you begin to **Change** that pattern, and a new you starts to **Evolve!**

In my pursuit of becoming an ACE, I take a moment to reflect on the qualities that make me powerful. These are how I decide to describe myself. While I am not perfect, I AM PERFECTLY ME!

Remember that the ACE is the highest ranked card in the suit and deck. ACES are powerful and you are now your most powerful self. Revel in your evolution and stand in the POWER OF ME!!

Take a moment to reflect on the qualities that make YOU powerful! What makes you an ACE? How do you describe yourself? Embrace and OWN the words you have chosen to define you!

_____
_____
_____
_____
_____
_____
_____
_____
_____
_____

CHAPTER 10

YOU ARE A W.O.W. Warrior!

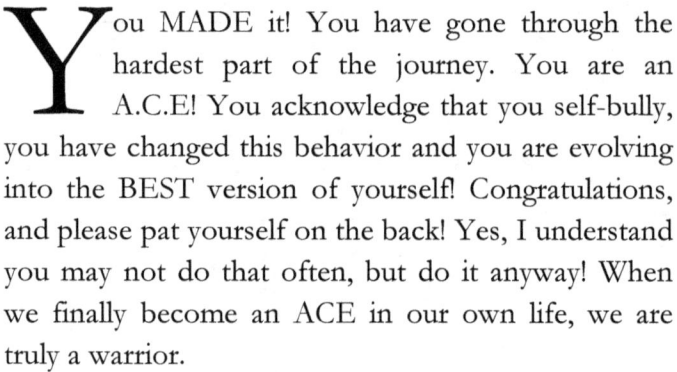

You MADE it! You have gone through the hardest part of the journey. You are an A.C.E! You acknowledge that you self-bully, you have changed this behavior and you are evolving into the BEST version of yourself! Congratulations, and please pat yourself on the back! Yes, I understand you may not do that often, but do it anyway! When we finally become an ACE in our own life, we are truly a warrior.

Here's a definition:

Warrior: a person who shows or has shown great vigor, courage, or aggressiveness.

If I could award you a crown, I would. We deserve one for conquering our words. It is no simple task to conquer years of old patterns of telling ourselves lies. Straighten your crown, stand up tall, and embrace the warrior you have become!

W.O.W. Warriors!

W - War

O - On

W - Words

It means you are a warrior in the War On Words. This is and always will be a continuing journey, a constant battle, and one we will all fight <u>together</u>. You will <u>never</u> be alone. We are all in community in this battle. Our words carry weight and can either weigh us down or give us wings and lift us up.

Speak love and light to yourself, to others but most of all to yourself. You are the boss, applesauce, and your word is the most important, next to God's. The old saying "you are not the boss of me" is 100% correct. I AM THE BOSS OF ME!

You have been destined to receive blessings and to be a blessing. He has already spoken His truth over you in the Bible. In Jeremiah 29:11 "For I know the plans I have for you," declares the Lord, "plans to prosper you and not to harm you, plans to give you hope and a future."

The future is yours to create! Be a fierce WOW WARRIOR! Put your foot down, affirm your worthiness with your words, deflect other's opinions who aren't kind, control who is in your tribe, and surround yourself with those who are supportive of you living your best life.

You are the BOSS of YOU! You are that perfect, never duplicated snowflake and you ARE an unrepeatable miracle!

Write it 10 times! I AM an unrepeatable MIRACLE!

1. _____
2. _____
3. _____
4. _____
5. _____
6. _____
7. _____
8. _____
9. _____
10. _____

www.ingramcontent.com/pod-product-compliance
Lightning Source LLC
Chambersburg PA
CBHW052112070526
44584CB00017B/2449